FEARLESS COMPETITORS

PARKOUR

I0876021

GAIL PARMAN

Enslow PUBLISHING

Please visit our website, www.enslow.com. For a free color catalog of all our high-quality books, call toll free 1-800-398-2504 or fax 1-877-980-4454

Published in 2027 by
Enslow Publishing
2544 Clinton Street
Buffalo, NY 14224

Copyright © 2027 by Enslow Publishing

All rights reserved.

Portions of this work were originally authored by Demi Jackson and published as *Daredevil Sports: Parkour*. All new material in this edition is authored by Gail Parman.

No part of this book may be reproduced by any means without the written permission of the publisher.

Cataloging-in-Publication Data
Names: Parman, Gail.
Title: Parkour / Gail Parman.
Description: Buffalo, NY : Enslow Publishing, 2027. | Series: Fearless competitors | Includes glossary and index.
Identifiers: ISBN 9781978548909 (pbk.) | ISBN 9781978548916 (library bound) | ISBN 9781978548923 (ebook)
Subjects: LCSH: Parkour--Juvenile literature. | Extreme sports--Juvenile literature.
Classification: LCC GV1068.P377 M674 2027 | DDC 796.046--dc23

Printed in China

Photos Credits: Cover, p. 1 Anton Vierietin/Shutterstock.com; p. 3 Gorgev/Shutterstock.com; p. 3, 4, 6, 8, 11, 12, 15, 16, 19, 20, 23, 24, 26, 28 (black background) Propakages/Shutterstock.com; p. 4 Vagengeim/Shutterstock.com; p. 6 Fernando Avendano/Shutterstock.com; p. 8 Wikipedia; p. 8 Ground Picture/Shutterstock.com; p. 10 Andrew Will/Shutterstock.com; p. 12 Harmony Video Production/Shutterstock.com; p. 14 PabloBenii/Shutterstock.com; p. 16 Jacob Lund/Shutterstock.com; p. 18 Alexandr Jitarev/Shutterstock.com; p. 20 areporter/Shutterstock.com; p. 22 Kiefer Photography/Shutterstock.com; p. 24 Enfoca y dispara/Shutterstock.com; p. 26 oneinchpunch/Shutterstock.com; p. 28 Aleks Images/Shutterstock.com; p. 30 Rommel Canlas/Shutterstock.com

CPSIA compliance information: Batch #QSENS27: For further information, contact Enslow Publishing, New York, New York, at 1-800-398-2504.

Find us on

Contents

OVER THE TOP

You're running fast. Your arms and legs are pumping, your heart is pounding, and sweat breaks out across your brow. A low wall stands in your way. Without losing speed, you brace your arms on top of the wall and push your body over it. This is parkour (pahr-KOOR).

FEARLESS FACTS

When most runners see an **obstacle** in their way, they go around it. But people who practice parkour learn how to move over obstacles safely and smoothly.

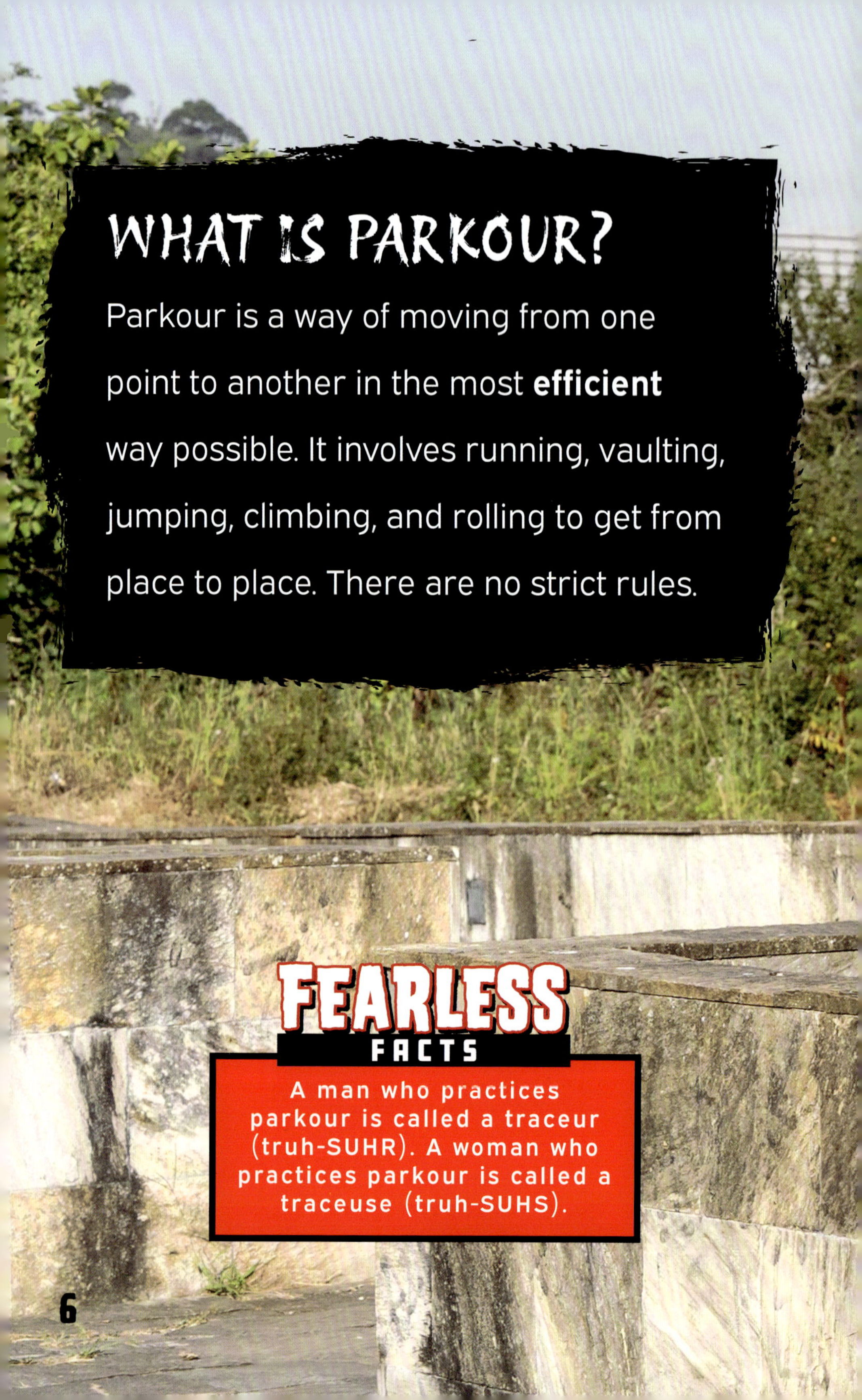

WHAT IS PARKOUR?

Parkour is a way of moving from one point to another in the most **efficient** way possible. It involves running, vaulting, jumping, climbing, and rolling to get from place to place. There are no strict rules.

FEARLESS FACTS

A man who practices parkour is called a traceur (truh-SUHR). A woman who practices parkour is called a traceuse (truh-SUHS).

PARKOUR'S BEGINNINGS

Parkour began in the 1980s and 1990s. It was invented by David Belle, a French actor and stuntman. His father, an **acrobat** and fireman, **inspired** Belle's movement style. Interest in parkour took off when people saw videos of Belle and his friends doing wild moves!

FEARLESS FACTS

Belle is known for his incredible parkour skills. He has jumped over cars, landed on thin railings after leaping over stairs, and even jumped between tall buildings!

Belle and his friends were more interested in getting better at parkour than spreading the word. So, it wasn't until the 2000s that parkour caught on in the United States. Parkour is still fairly new in the U.S., but it's catching on quickly, especially among teens and young adults.

FEARLESS FACTS

Even today, parkour is much more popular in Europe than in the United States.

Today, parkour is a growing sport. Parkour clubs have begun in cities across the world. You can practice parkour almost anywhere! Some cities are building special parks for the athletes who want to practice it.

FEARLESS FACTS

Not everyone sees parkour as a good thing. Some worry it can be dangerous for athletes and may even damage property.

WHAT IS FREERUNNING?

Sometimes parkour is called "freerunning." Traceur Sebastien Foucan first created the word to describe parkour to people who speak English. But over time, freerunning has become its own separate **discipline**. Like traceurs, freerunners run, jump, and climb through their neighborhoods.

FEARLESS FACTS

Some people define parkour as the most efficient way from point to point, while freerunning is the most creative way from point to point.

Freerunning and parkour are similar, but they have one key difference. Freerunners value creativity above all. It often includes flips and other **gymnastics** moves. On the other hand, parkour is about overcoming obstacles with minimal movement and maximum speed!

FEARLESS FACTS

Parkour is popular among fearless athletes. It requires both physical and **mental** strength.

GETTING STARTED

If you're interested in learning parkour, you won't be running up walls the first day! A lot of classes teach the ideas behind parkour first. They want to inspire new traceurs to see the world as a playground, whether it's a park or the streets in their neighborhood.

FEARLESS FACTS

New traceurs start with basic jumps and vaults and learn to land safely. It's important to start gradually.

GEAR UP

The only gear you need for parkour is a pair of sneakers with good grip on the bottom. Knee pads are also a good idea for beginners! You can wear what you want when doing parkour. Loose-fitting clothing is often recommended because it lets you move easily.

FEARLESS FACTS

No special equipment needed—traceurs vault over fences and scale brick walls using just their own bodies!

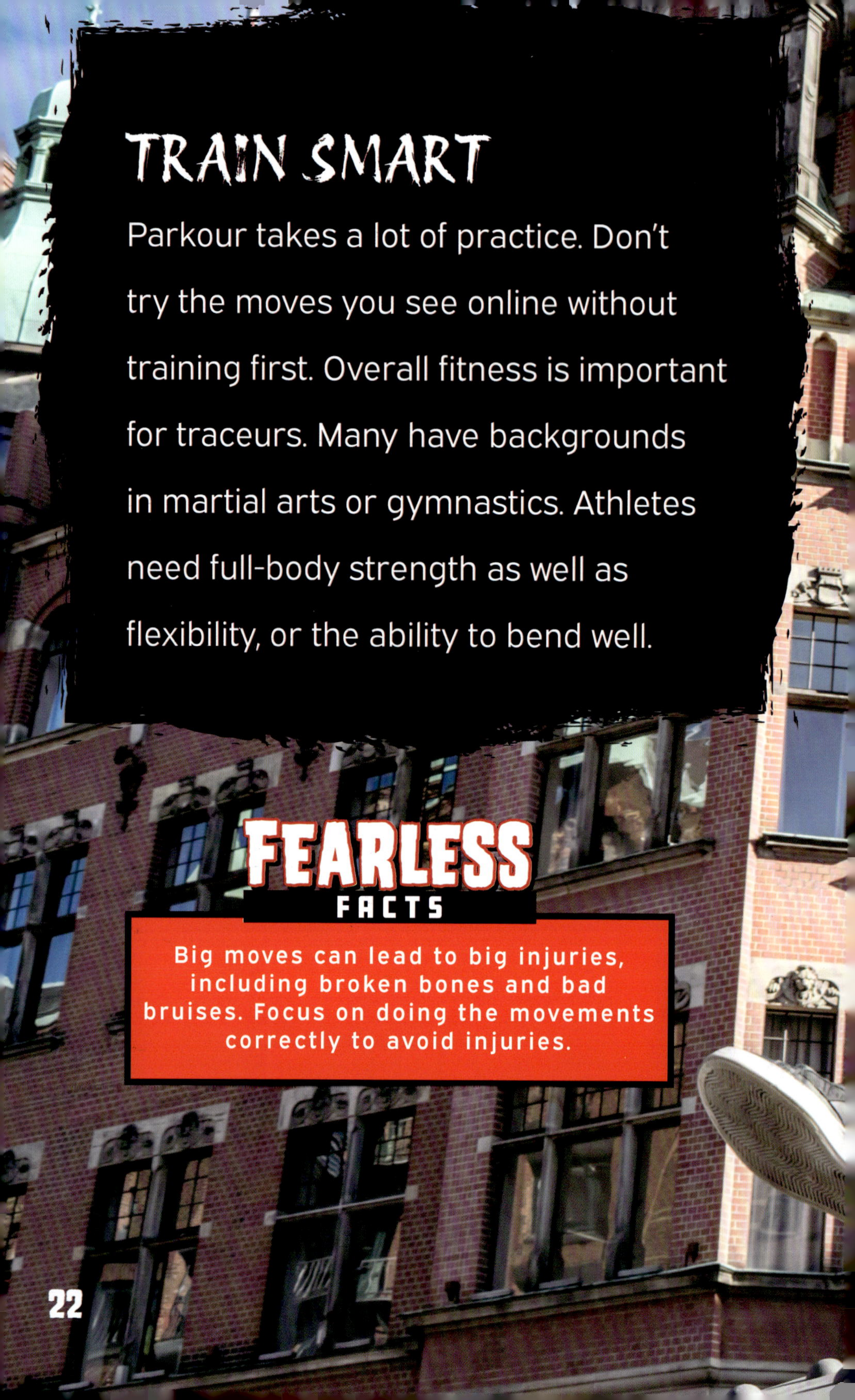

TRAIN SMART

Parkour takes a lot of practice. Don't try the moves you see online without training first. Overall fitness is important for traceurs. Many have backgrounds in martial arts or gymnastics. Athletes need full-body strength as well as flexibility, or the ability to bend well.

FEARLESS FACTS

Big moves can lead to big injuries, including broken bones and bad bruises. Focus on doing the movements correctly to avoid injuries.

Parkour uses many different movements. A parkour roll is when the traceur rolls to soften landings from high jumps. A wall run is when the traceur jumps and pushes off a wall to reach the top. A precision jump means jumping and landing accurately with both feet.

FEARLESS FACTS

These moves take a lot of practice! Many parkour moves are practiced close to the ground first.

TOUGH COMPETITION

Parkour athletes don't usually compete against each other. It is more about competing against themselves and pushing their own limits. Traceurs learn to overcome obstacles and their own fears. Some people even consider parkour to be a form of movement art.

FEARLESS FACTS

How fast can you move across your backyard without touching the grass? Trying parkour may help you find new strength and creativity you didn't know you had!

TOW-AWAY
NO STOPPING
ANY TIME
110
Fwy

GET CREATIVE!

Parkour is great for the mind and body. It helps develop strength, coordination, problem-solving skills, and confidence. In parkour, you need to think fast to adapt to the changing environment. It teaches you to push yourself and shows you just how much you're capable of!

FEARLESS FACTS

Today, you can find classes teaching parkour to all ages. Some gyms are set up specifically for doing parkour.

Safety First

ALL PARKOUR ATHLETES SHOULD:

- master basic moves before trying anything harder.
- try new moves on the ground or low walls first.
- learn how to land safely. A good landing is a quiet one.
- wear shoes that fit well and have bottoms with a good grip.
- stay fit in other ways, like running or yoga.
- be mindful of where they practice, watching out for cars and other people.

For More Information

BOOKS

Laughlin, Kara L. *Parkour.* The Child's World, 2018.

Loye, Lily. *Parkour.* DiscoverRoo, 2021.

Waxman, Laura Hamilton. *Ninja Competitions.* Lerner Publications, 2020.

WEBSITES

What is Parkour? A Kids' Guide to Running, Jumping, and Climbing
https://englishnewsforkids.com/what-is-parkour-a-kids-guide-to-running-jumping-and-climbing/
Learn more about parkour, then take a short quiz to test your knowledge!

Parkour Facts for Kids
https://kids.kiddle.co/Parkour
Learn more about parkour, including its key principles.

Publisher's note to educators and parents: Our editors have carefully reviewed these websites to ensure that they are suitable for students. Many websites change frequently, however, and we cannot guarantee that a site's future contents will continue to meet our high standards of quality and educational value. Be advised that students should be closely supervised whenever they access the Internet.

Glossary

acrobat: someone who performs gymnastics

discipline: a kind of training

efficient: having to do with the most effective or purposeful way of doing something

gymnastics: a sport that includes rolls, flips, and other moves often performed on rings or bars

inspire: to cause someone to want to do something

mental: having to do with the mind

obstacle: something that blocks a path

Index